TRUST
ME

THIS IS A TRAVELING BUK...yes BUK,
which is a short but impactful read.

INSTRUCTIONS BEFORE READING THIS BUK.

~ I need your help to HEAL AMERICA

~ Read this 5 to 10 minute buk today.

~ Sign and date

~ Pass your buk to someone else to read, sign, date, and pass on.

~ REPEAT THIS PROCESS ALL OVER AMERICA

Note: If you don't want to pass your buk on then tell others about it or simply order another copy at www.drhlbarner.com or Amazon.

Sign Name	State/City	Date	(Optional) Occupation
_____			
_____			

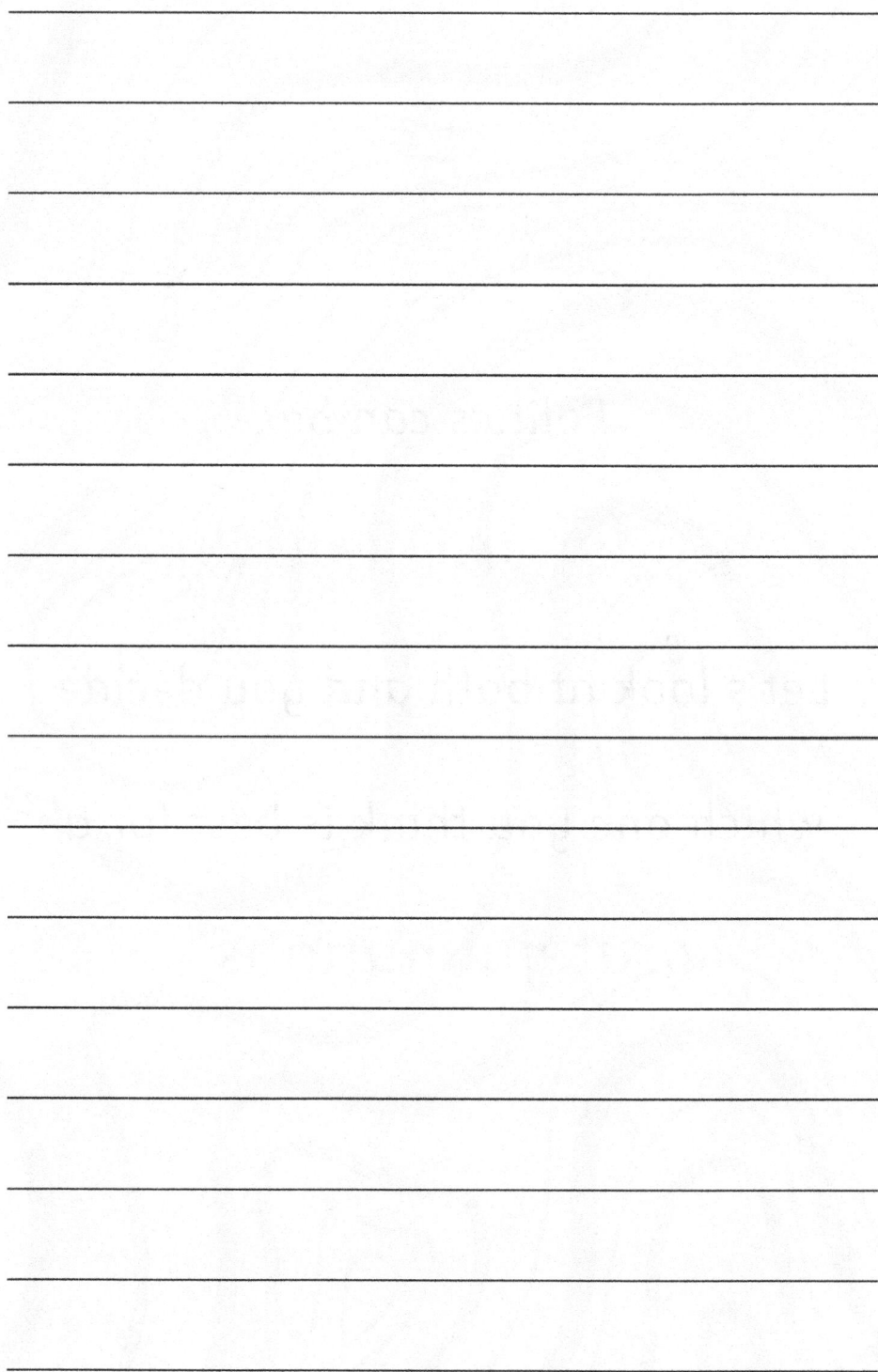

Politics can be

Godly or Un-godly.

Let's look at both and you decide

which one you think is best for a

grateful nations.

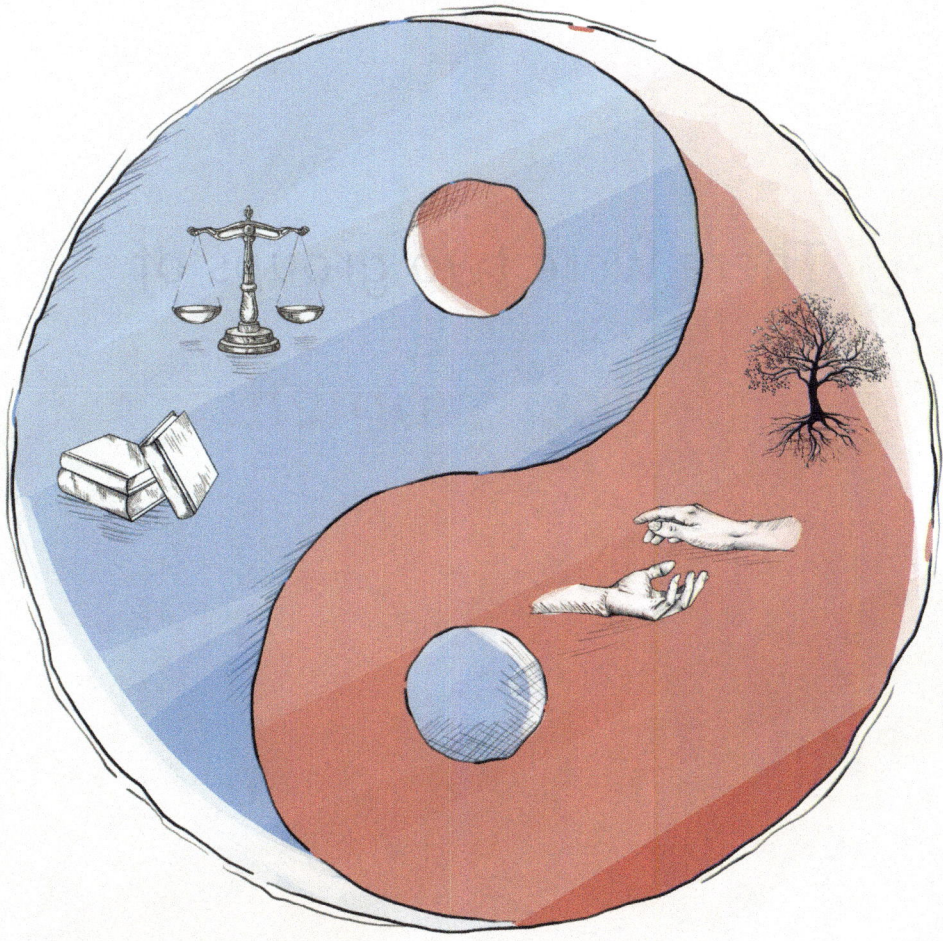

There were two groups of

men & women.

One group favor

Red.

The other group favor

blue.

Both groups were put in a room with a table filled with lots of food.

They had an enough food to last 60 days. The food was from all over the world. The best foods from the best restaurants. Fruits, vegetables, steaks, fish, ham, drinks, water, deserts, and much more.

They were tasked to come

up with ideas to heal a

divided country.

These two groups were Partisan.

They hated each other. They didn't

trust each other. They refused

to work together.

They were locked

in a room for

30 days.

Do not Disturb
meeting in progress

Day after day they went

without food.

At the end of 30 days,

we unlocked the door

to see how things

were going.

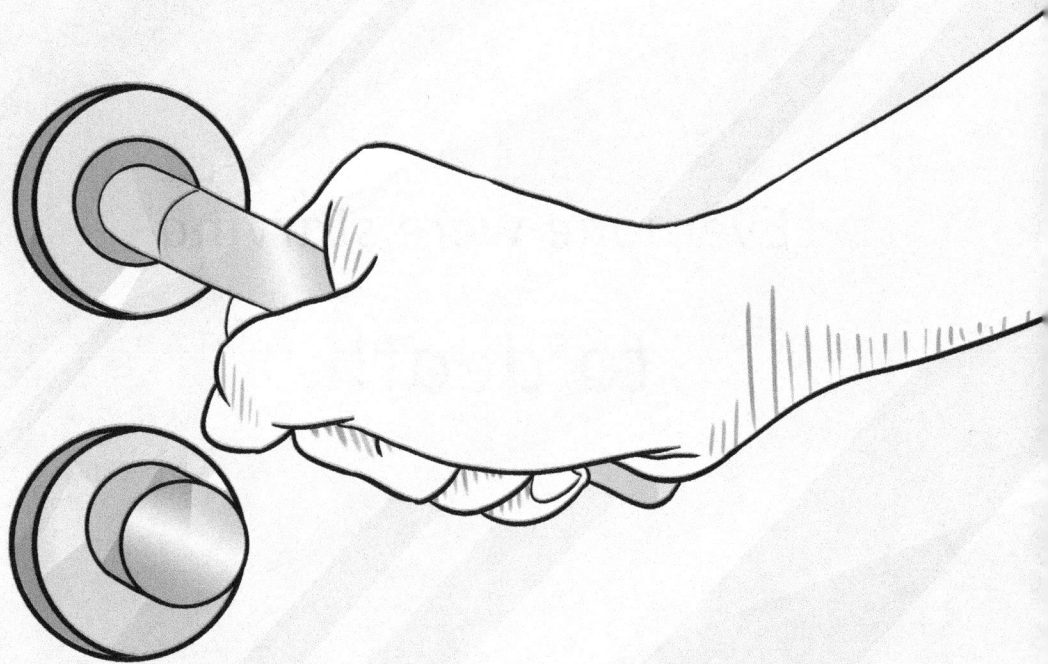

Everyone were starving

to death.

Why were they starving

to death

if they had all that

wonderful food

in the room?

There hands and arms

were made of

Spoons and Folks.

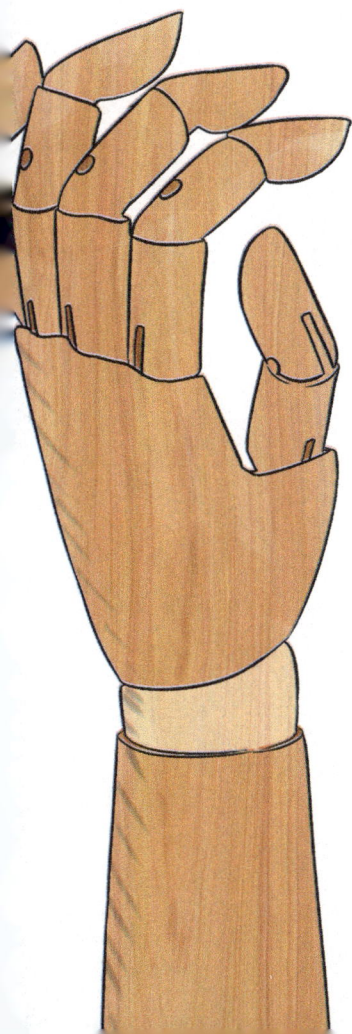

They couldn't **bend their arms** to feed themselves.

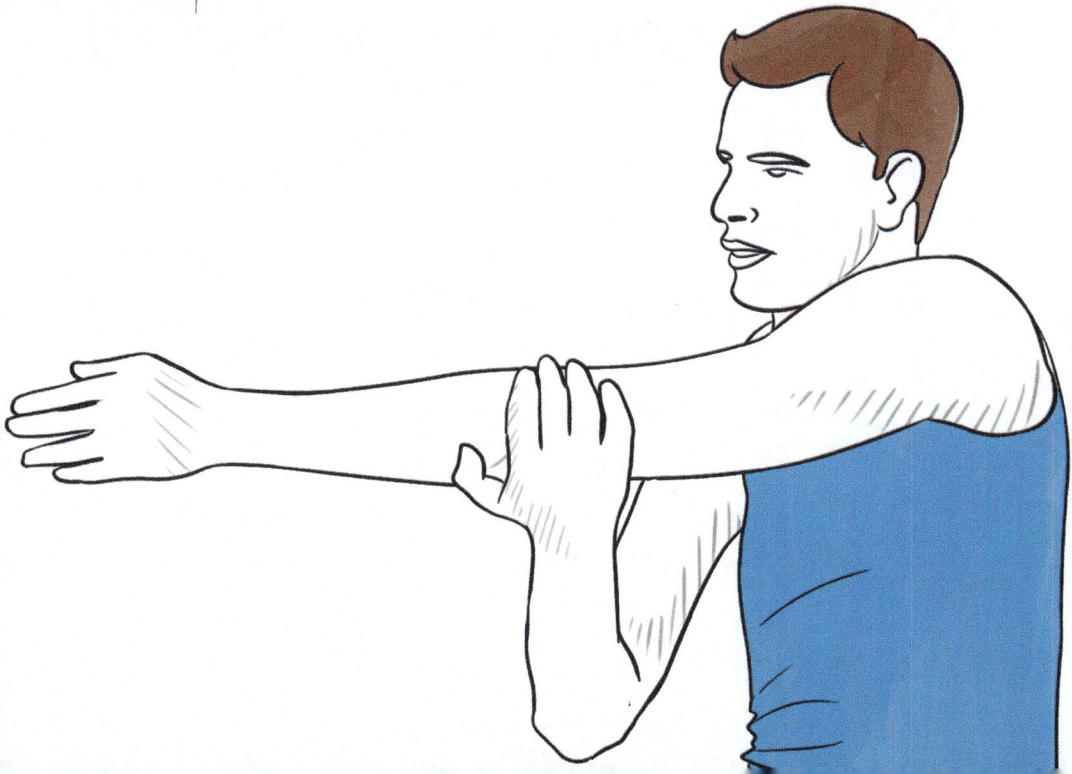

They couldn't agree on any

ideas to heal the country.

So the country parished.

Then we selected two more

groups of people.

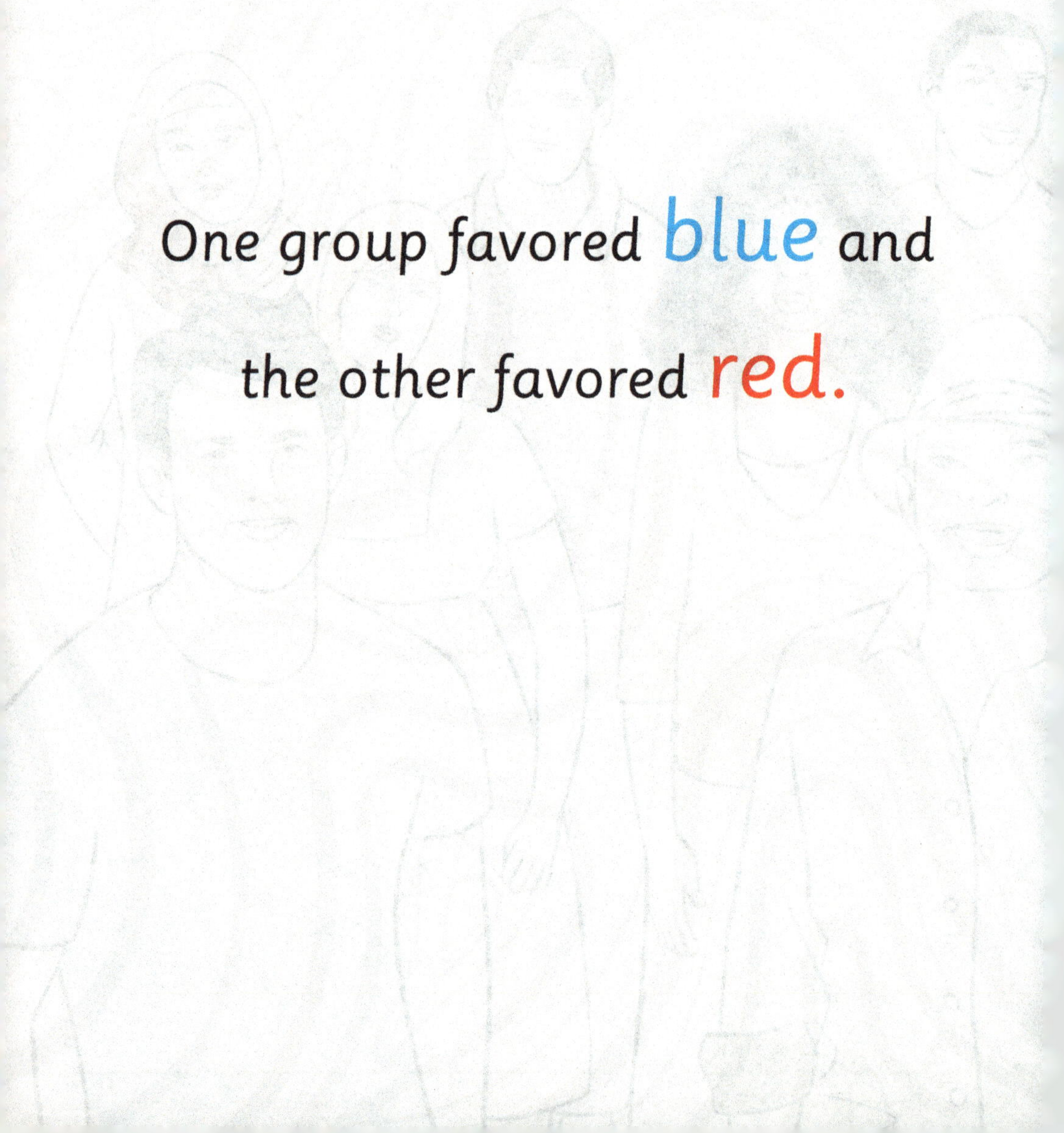

One group favored blue and

the other favored red.

They too were placed in a room

with the same food.

They too had an enough food to last 60 days. The food was from all over the world. The best foods from the best restaurants.

Fruits, vegetables, steaks, fish, ham, drinks, water, deserts, and much more.

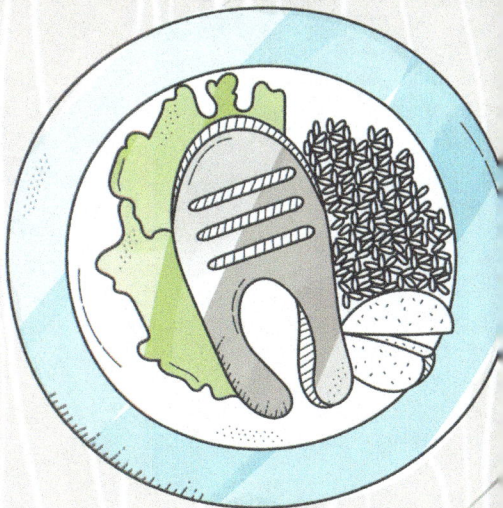

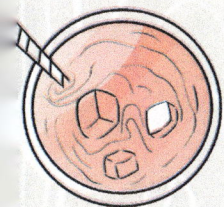

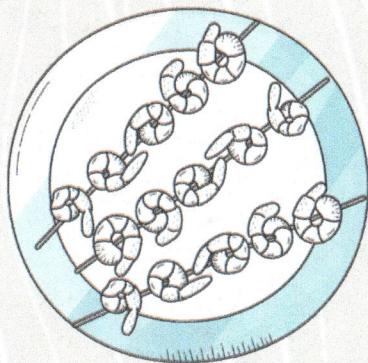

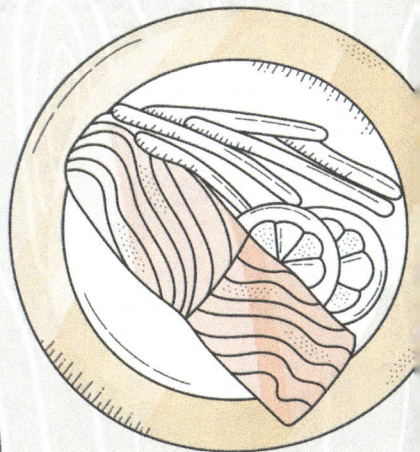

They were tasked to heal the

same divided country.

These two groups were bi-partisan.

They respected each other.

They wanted to work with

each other. They wanted to

heal the country.

Also, they were locked in a

room for 30 days.

They agreed that they would be

stronger together, so they

put the country first.

Day after day went by and they

worked hard and enjoyed

great meals together.

After 30 days we unlocked the

door to see how things

were going.

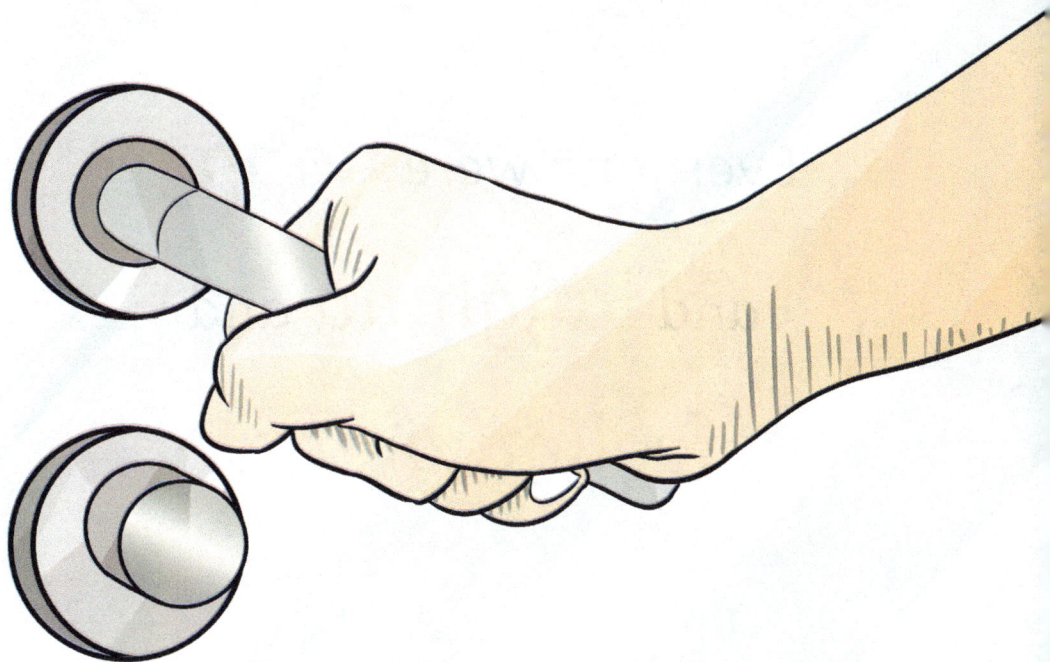

Everyone were happy

and laughing and

feeling great.

They were able to eat. They were happy. They were excited and full of life.

There hands & arms were made of Spoons & Folks just like the other group.

This **new group** couldn't

bend their arms

to feed themselves either.

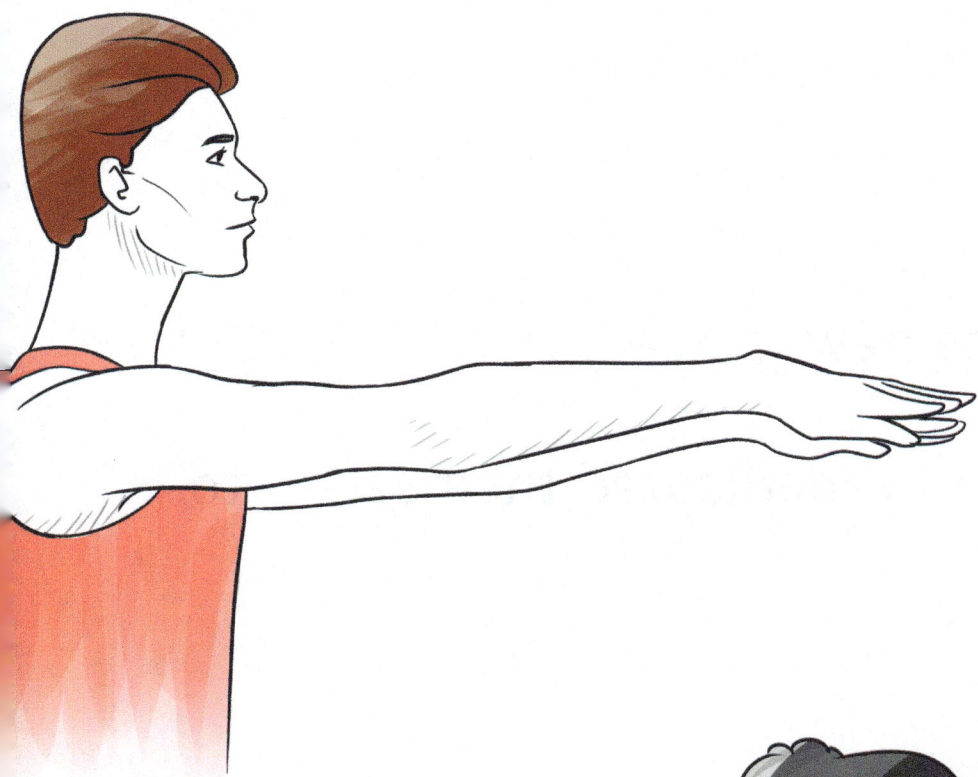

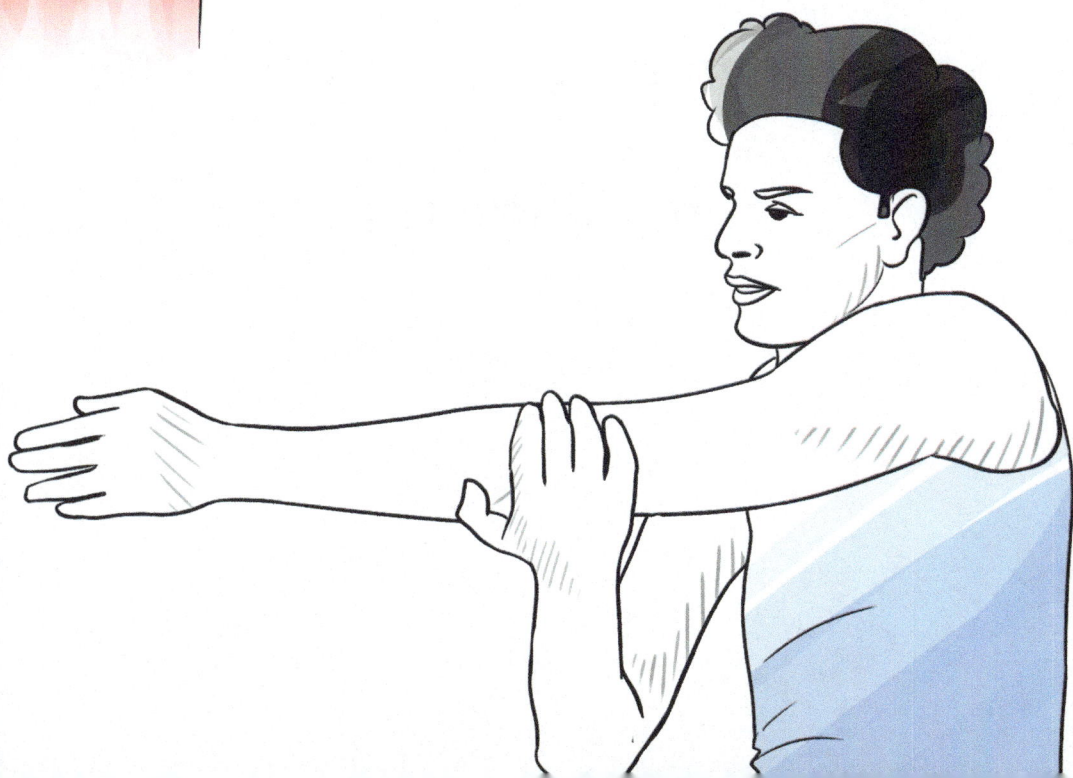

The new group prayed together

rededicated themselves to

God.

And then they allowed God

to do the rest.

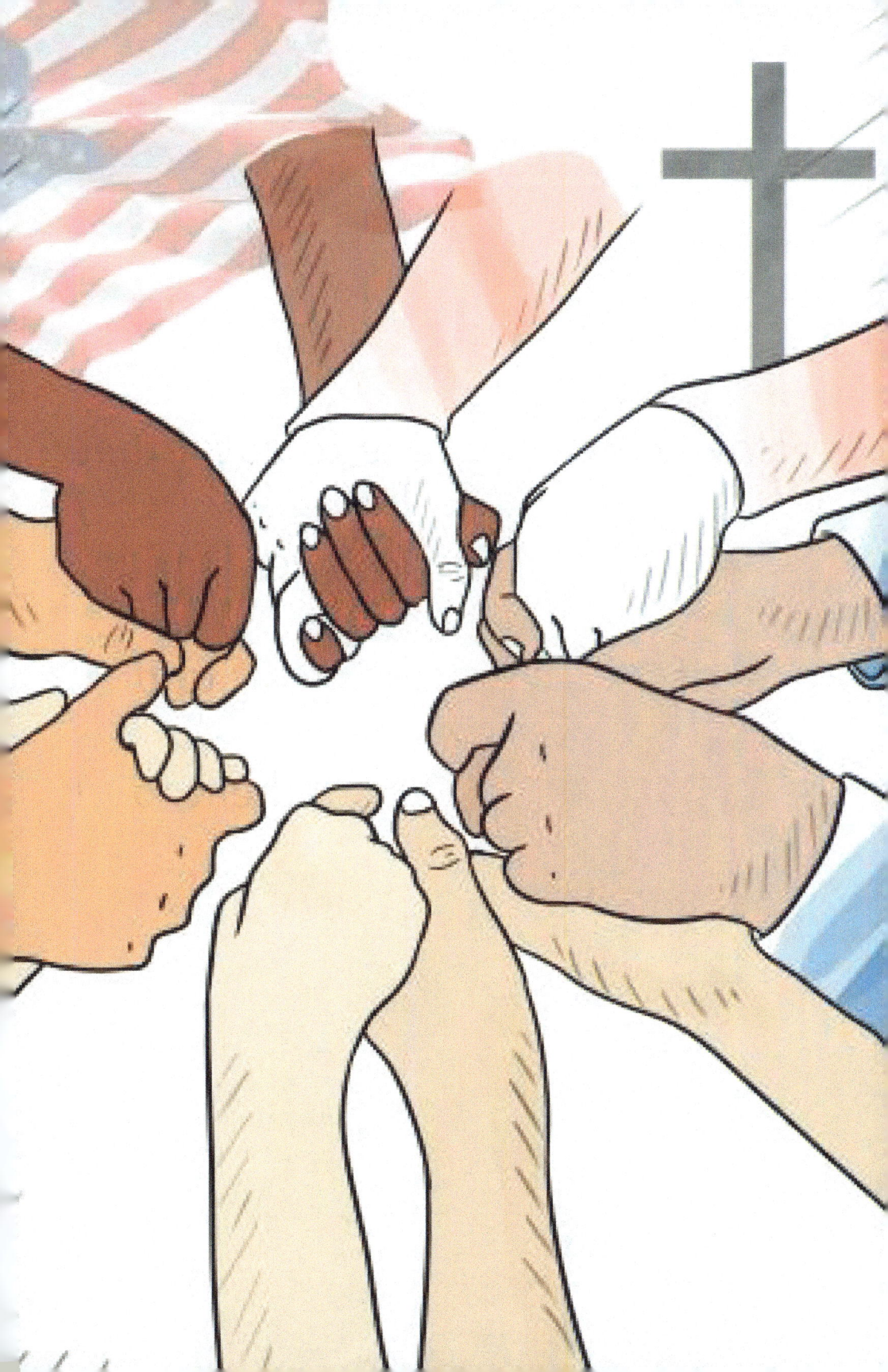

How were they able to eat if their arms & hands were made of spoons & folks and couldn't bend them to feed themselves.

They fed one another!

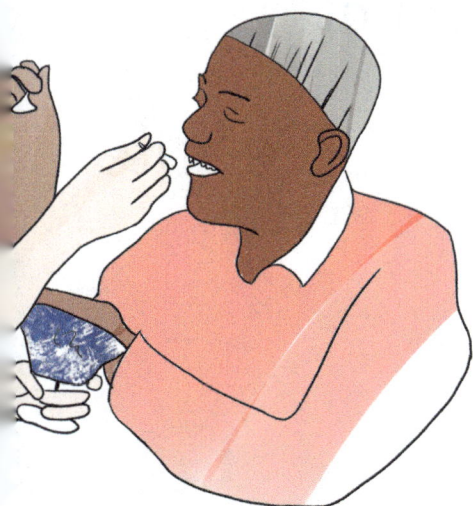

There is room at

God's table for ALL People.

All hands are needed in

God's Kingdom.

Let's practice on earth.

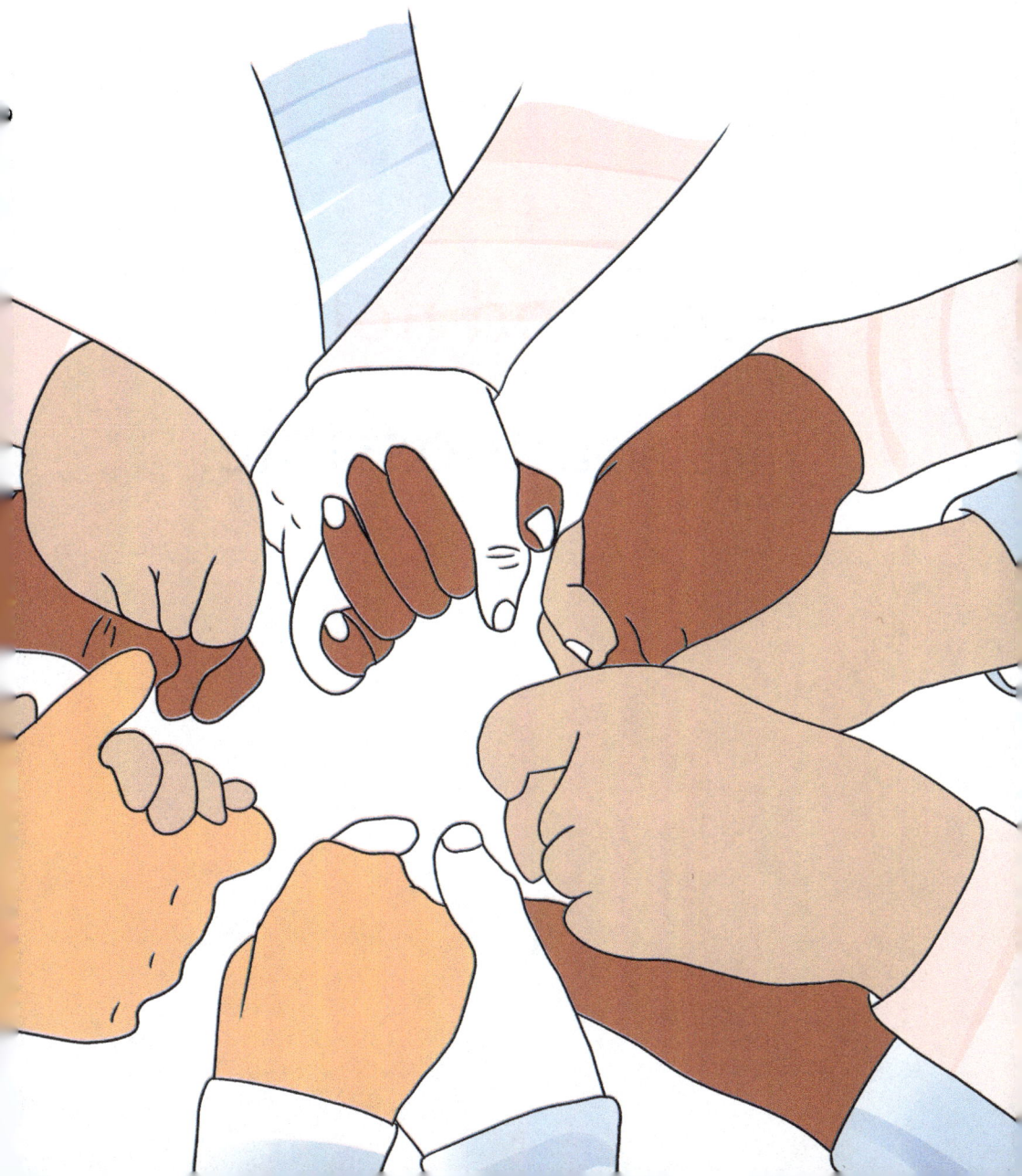

For with God nothing

shall be impossible.

First edition
ISBN: 978-1-952321-05-4

ABOUT THE AUTHOR:

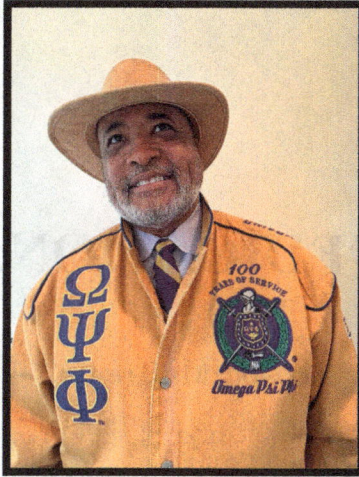

Dr. Honney Lavern Barner grew up in Portsmouth, Virginia. Growing up without his Father he looked to his mother and grandfather for moral and spiritual guidance. His mother eventually led him to Jesus Christ and his grandfather continued to encourage his spiritual journey. As a young adult, he developed a passion for attending different churches and local revivals. He enjoyed the preaching and teaching of the Gospel of Jesus Christ and was determined to learn everything he could about Him. Once he learned that every human being regardless of color, race, sex, religion, ethic group, rich, poor or political preference, is a child of the most high God and his life changed forever.

DEDICATION:

To God, My Creator.

Jesus Christ, My Lord and Savior.

The Holy Spirit, My Guide and Comforter.

To every human being, past, present, and future.

ACKNOWLEDGEMENTS:

To my mother and grandfather who lead me to Christ.

To all the Pastors, Teachers, Evangelists, Apostles,
and Prophets who called to share the Word of God.

To all the men and women who are disciples.

Ephesians 4:4-6 "There is one body, and one Spirit, even as ye are
called in one hope of your calling; One Lord, one faith, one
baptism; One God, and Father of all, who is above all, and through
all, and in you all."

Books vs. BUKs

B - Brief
U - Useful/Utilitarian
K - Knowledge

This acronym emphasizes the essence of the reading material being brief, focused on utility, and providing essential knowledge. The aim is to create a reading experience that is time-efficient, purposeful, and conducive to retaining information. Additionally, the incorporation of graphics enhances the learning process and aids in better comprehension and retention. The BUKs are designed to cut through the unnecessary details, offering a streamlined and impactful reading experience that empowers readers to quickly absorb and apply the key insights.

A Call to Action

Dr. HL Barner's vision for BUKs is not just a novel idea; it's a call to action for a more efficient, impactful, and accessible approach to learning. Whether you're a busy professional, a lifelong learner, or someone seeking quick and practical knowledge, BUKs are poised to be the catalyst for a positive change in the way we consume and apply information. Embrace the BUK revolution – where learning is no longer a cumbersome task but a liberating experience that empowers you to take swift and informed action.

BARNER

ENTERPRISES, LLC

THANK YOU FROM OUR FAMILY TO YOURS.

Made in the USA
Monee, IL
12 March 2024